THAT YOU MIGHT HAVE LIFE

An Introduction to the Paschal Mystery of Christ

WORKBOOK

THAT YOU MIGHT HAVE LIFE

An Introduction to the Paschal Mystery of Christ

WORKBOOK

TAN Books
Gastonia, North Carolina

Compiled by Melissa Girard

Series design by Margaret Ryland

Cover and layout by Caroline Green

Cover image: *The Ascension*, Giovanni Bernardino Azzolino (1572–1645)

ISBN: 978-1-5051-1939-8

Published in the United States by
TAN Books
PO Box 269
Gastonia, NC 28053
www.TANBooks.com

Printed in the United States of America

CONTENTS

A Note to Instructors

As Pope St. John Paul II made clear in his apostolic exhortation *Catechesi Tradendae*, "The definitive aim of catechesis is to put people not only in touch but in communion, in intimacy, with Jesus Christ."

The *Formed in Christ* series seeks to fulfill this call, fostering intimacy with Christ through its dynamic content.

Rather than presenting religion as any other subject to be mastered, our series editors have designed each text to plumb the bottomless genius of Catholicism found in centuries of theologians, saints, councils, and papal teachings.

The six volumes in *Formed in Christ* cover every point in the USCCB's guidelines for high school catechesis.

In *That You Might Have Life*, the course of study will unpack God's plan for humanity from "the beginning," and how that plan was revealed after man's fall from grace. It will chronicle God's covenant with Israel and the words of the prophets until it reached its fulfillment in the life, death, and resurrection of Jesus Christ. Lastly, it will examine how each of us enter into that plan through a life of discipleship.

This supplemental workbook is designed to provide instructors with test material and direction for enhancing students' grasp of the material.

For each chapter, the following components are included:

Memory Verse

Appealing not only to the head but also the heart, a suitable memory verse, chosen for its relation to the chapter's content, is suggested to help the student with his or her prayer life. Throughout the week, have your student attempt to recite this verse from memory.

Key Terms

A list of key terms from the chapter is included. Students are encouraged to write down some notes about these terms (either here in the workbook or in a separate notebook), using not only the text but the *Catechism of the Catholic Church* and a good Catholic dictionary as well. This will not only prepare students for testing but deepen their understanding of the content.

Questions for Review

Taken directly from the student text, the Questions for Review, provided in "short answer" format, ensure comprehension of the material. Answers are provided in the back.

Quiz

For each chapter, ten questions are provided for testing. Multiple Choice, True or False, and Fill-in-the-Blank quizzes vary throughout the workbook. Answers are provided in the back.

Questions for Discussion

Dialogue between students and instructors is essential. Not only will the Questions for Discussion (included both here and in the student text) provide another opportunity for reinforcing the material, but the questions are specifically designed to prompt students to reflect on their own faith experience. While discussion between students and instructors is highly recommended, the Questions for Discussion can also be used as prompts for personal writing exercises. Since these are more for personal reflection, no answers are provided.

Essay Topics and / or Further Study

The *Formed in Christ* series is designed to expose students to Church documents and the writings of theologians from all stages of Church history. But these selected readings are just the beginning of Catholic thought that students can discover. The Essay Topics and/or Further Study suggestions encourage students to dig deeper into the wealth of Catholic teaching through independent study. A mix of personal, subjective prompts and research topics, these suggestions will enable your student to learn more about their Catholic faith. Grading is left up to the instructor's discretion.

Final Exam

In the back, you will find a final exam that aggregates all the most important content. This provides a barometer for how well your student(s) absorbed the material. It consists of matching and short answer. Answers are provided in the back.

Part I

THE GOODNESS OF CREATION
AND OUR FALL FROM GRACE

The Creation of the World and Our First Parents

Memory Verse

> In the beginning God created the heavens and the earth. The earth was without form and void, and darkness was upon the face of the deep; and the Spirit of God was moving over the face of the waters.
>
> —Genesis 1:1–2

Key Terms

Genesis

Creation

Figurative language

Symbolic language

Form

Order

Logos

Material universe

Angels

Questions for Review

1. What questions does the creation account in Genesis seek to answer? What questions does it not seek to answer?

2. What do we mean when we say God is the creator of all things "visible and invisible"?

3. Through whom did God create the world?

4. Who created God?

5. What are angels?

Quiz

1. The creation accounts of Genesis convey:
   A. scientific facts.
   B. religious truths.
   C. historical details.

2. Theological truths are conveyed in Genesis through:
   A. fiction.
   B. figurative language.
   C. folklore.

3. Science cannot answer questions about:
   A. creation.
   B. living beings.
   C. our purpose.

4. Creation reveals the _____ of the universe.
   A. chaos
   B. void
   C. order

5. God began to order the universe first by creating:
   A. light and darkness.
   B. sky and seas.
   C. heavens and the earth.

6. All things were made *through*:
   A. the Father.
   B. the Son.
   C. the Holy Spirit.

7. *Logos* is the source word for:
   A. logic.
   B. ontological.
   C. creating.

8. The material universe includes:
   A. spiritual realities.
   B. God himself.
   C. time and space.

9. _____ is uncreated.
   A. The universe
   B. God
   C. An angel

10. Angels comes from the Greek word *angelos*, meaning:
    A. "messenger."
    B. "pure being."
    C. "servant."

Questions for Discussion

1. What are some examples of questions science can't answer? What does this teach us about the limits of science?

2. When you look around at the created world, what evidence do you see for God's existence?

3. What does it mean that God has given order to creation? What are some of the consequences of this?

Essay Questions / Further Study

1. What scientific research about the creation of the universe can you find that is compatible with the Catholic understanding? While science cannot tell us about spiritual realities, does it give you further insight into God's plan for humanity?

2. Give some examples of realities or phenomena in the universe that point to its order. Can these examples tell us anything about the divine mind?

3. Using the Catechism, study what the Church teaches about creation. How was each Person of the Trinity involved in the work of creation?

4. What is the difference between physical and spiritual realities? Why is it so important to accept that God is the creator of both?

Human Beings

The Summit of Creation

Memory Verse

> What is man that you are mindful of him,
> And the son of man that you visit him?
> For you have made him a little lower than the angels,
> And you have crowned him with glory and honor.
> You have made him to have dominion over the works of your hands.

—Psalm 8:4–6

Key Terms

Dignity

Dominion

Communion of divine persons

Communion of human persons

Marriage

Chastity

Communion of friendship

Soul

Harmony

Original justice

Questions for Review

1. What does it mean for man to be a steward of creation?

2. What sets the human person apart from all the other creatures of the earth?

3. How do married persons and families image God?

4. A human person is a perfect union of what two things?

5. What do we call the original state of harmony that existed in the Garden?

Quiz

1. Unlike every other creature, only _____ reflect God's immortality, rationality, and freedom.

2. God gave man _____ to rule over creation.

3. _____ is purely spiritual, and neither male nor female.

4. Mother, father, and children reflect the Trinity, a _____ that is united in generous and life-giving love.

5. _____ frees us from being overpowered by sexual passions.

6. Man's _____ comes immediately from God and does not break down after death but is immortal.

7. Alone among creatures, man is both a _____ and _____ being.

8. Pope St. John Paul II wrote that the body "expresses _____."

9. Before sin entered the Garden, man and woman experienced _____ with each other, creation, and within themselves.

10. Before the Fall, God made it so that doing the right thing was easy and natural. This state is called _____.

Questions for Discussion

1. What are some ways we can be good stewards of creation?

2. If every person is the image of God, what does that tell us about how we should treat one another?

3. Have you seen the differences between men and women divide us? How have you seen the differences between us unite us and help us?

Essay Topics / Further Study

1. Because humans alone are created in the image and likeness of God, what do we reveal about who God is? What are ways that we act *against* the image and likeness of God?

2. Understanding men and women's uniqueness in all of creation, why is it significant that God gave us dominion to rule over the world? In what ways do you see that dominion being exercised properly? What ways is that dominion abused?

3. Find a religious community whose work with the goods of creation reflects good stewardship. Compare their life of work and prayer to the work and prayer of Adam and Eve before the Fall.

4. Explain how the family reflects the life of the Trinity. Give examples of how you see the Trinity reflected in your own family. In what ways can you personally strive to show generous and life-giving love?

5. Research what some of the early Church Fathers taught about original holiness, original justice, and life before sin entered the Garden of Eden.

The Fall from Grace: Original Sin

Memory Verse

‖ For if many died through one man's trespass, much more have the grace of God and the free gift in the grace of that one man Jesus Christ abounded for many.

—Romans 5:15

Key Terms

Satan

Demons

Tree of Knowledge of Good and Evil

Free will

Sanctifying grace

Original sin

Concupiscence

Savior

Questions for Review

1. Who is Satan?

2. What did Satan promise Adam and Eve?

3. What did Adam and Eve lose when they disobeyed God?

4. What do we call the sin of our first parents and the fallen state of human nature inherited from them?

5. After announcing their punishment for sin, what good news does God give Adam and Eve?

Quiz

True/False

1. ____ Our first parents were created in friendship with God, but they lost that friendship through sin.
2. ____ Satan is a fallen angel who temporarily disobeyed God his creator.
3. ____ Before the Fall, Adam and Eve were free from sin but not suffering and death.
4. ____ The tree of the knowledge of good and evil is a symbol of the boundaries placed on man by God.
5. ____ God gives us free will knowing we have the choice to reject him.
6. ____ The serpent told Eve that the fruit of the tree of knowledge of good and evil would make her like God.
7. ____ Spiritual death is the loss of one's soul.
8. ____ All of humanity is descended from one couple.

9. ____ Original sin affects everyone after the age of reason.

10. ____ The inclination toward sin is called original sin.

Questions for Discussion

1. Satan tempted Adam and Eve with a promise that they "could be like God." Today, he continues to tempt people to "play God" and make up a moral law for themselves. Can you think of some examples of people "playing God"? Why is this so dangerous?

2. Because we are all interconnected, both our good and bad actions affect others. Can you think of some examples of how our personal bad choices hurt those around us? What about our good personal choices? How do they help those around us?

3. Because of original sin, we often don't do the good things we know we ought to do. Do you see this tendency in yourself or your friends sometimes? Give one example of this from your personal experience.

Essay Topics / Further Study

1. Write a modern retelling of the tempting of Adam and Eve. What would Satan use today to lead a man or woman to sin?

2. Make a diagram of what life was like for Adam and Eve before and after the Fall. What characteristics, or supernatural virtues, did they have and lose? What effects would sin have had on their everyday lives?

3. With the Gospel in mind, what elements of the story of Adam and Eve foreshadow the coming of the promised Savior? In what ways is Adam a "type" of Jesus? In what ways is Eve a "type" of Mary?

4. Do further research on original sin. What does the Catechism say? Does our understanding of original sin shed more light on the practice of infant Baptism? Why?

5. Define concupiscence. How do you see the effects of concupiscence in your own life? What about in greater society, and in large human institutions?

Part II

THE PROMISE OF A MESSIAH

The First Prophecy of the Messiah

Memory Verse

> Then the Lord God said to the woman, "What is this that you have done?" The woman said, "The serpent beguiled me, and I ate." The Lord God said to the serpent, "Because you have done this, cursed are you above all cattle, and above all wild animals; upon your belly you shall go, and dust you shall eat all the days of your life. I will put enmity between you and the woman, and between your seed and her seed; he shall bruise your head, and you shall bruise his heel."
>
> —Genesis 3:13–15

Key Terms

Enmity

Protoevangelium

Seed

New Adam

New Eve

Cain

Babel

Questions for Review

1. What is the "protoevangelium"?

2. Why does the Church call Jesus the "New Adam"?

3. Why does the Church call Mary the "New Eve"?

4. What is the first way we see sin escalate after the fall of Adam and Eve?

5. What does the Tower of Babel symbolize?

Quiz

1. In Genesis 3:15, God promises to put _____ between Satan and "the woman."
   A. barriers
   B. grace
   C. enmity

2. The "first gospel" is called:
   A. the Gospel of Matthew.
   B. the proclamation.
   C. the protoevangelium.

3. The word _____ is a reference to a specific descendant of the woman.
   A. "protoevangelium"
   B. "generator"
   C. "seed"

4. Salvation comes through one man, whom we refer to as the:
   A. New Adam.
   B. Child.
   C. Seed.

5. Salvation occurs with the cooperation of:
   A. all peoples.
   B. the Patriarchs.
   C. Mary.

6. _____ was preserved from both original sin and personal sin.
   A. Eve
   B. Mary
   C. Cain

7. _____ becomes an opportunity for God to unveil a plan of love and mercy.
   A. Sin
   B. Prophecy
   C. The Bible

8. After the Fall, we see sin escalate, beginning with:
   A. the sins of Sodom and Gomorra.
   B. the sin of pride with the Tower of Babel.
   C. the sins of Cain.

9. The Tower of Babel is a manifestation of:
   A. ingenuity.
   B. jealousy.
   C. pride.

10. With Noah, God begins making a series of _____ that slowly unveil his plan.
    A. covenants
    B. proclamations
    C. punishments

Questions for Discussion

1. From the beginning, God has brought good out of sorrow. Have you ever experienced God bringing something good out of a bad situation in your life? Describe.

2. Great good came into the world because Jesus and Mary cooperated with God's plan for our redemption. They said yes to him. What is one way you can say yes to God today?

3. After Adam and Eve fell, their sin quickly escalated. Have you ever seen one sin lead to another, and then another? Describe.

Essay Topics / Further Study

1. Research what the Fathers of the Church teach about the similarities between Adam and Eve and Jesus and Mary. List all of the ways that Adam and Eve prepare us to understand the mission of Jesus and Mary.

2. We see the dramatic escalation of sin when Adam and Eve's firstborn son, Cain, commits the sins of jealousy, lying, lack of concern for one's neighbor, and murder. Find an example of a hardened sinner who experienced a conversion. What sins did they commit, and how did their former life of sin change their attitude once they chose to be faithful to Christ? Why are these dramatic conversion stories so important to share?

3. Mary's role in salvation is an important aspect of God's plan. Speak to a family member or friend who has a strong devotion to the Blessed Mother. How do they view Mary's role in the work of salvation?

4. We believe that Mary was preserved from both original sin and all personal sin. Using your Catechism or other resources of your choosing, read more about the Blessed Mother. What can we learn from her example, even though we experience the effects of sin?

5. Reread the story of the Tower of Babel in Genesis 11:1–9. Write a news article describing the events. Invent "eyewitnesses" to discuss.

The Promise Fulfilled

Memory Verse

Think not that I have come to abolish the law and the prophets; I have come not to abolish them but to fulfil them. For truly, I say to you, till heaven and earth pass away, not an iota, not a dot, will pass from the law until all is accomplished. Whoever then relaxes one of the least of these commandments and teaches men so, shall be called least in the kingdom of heaven; but he who does them and teaches them shall be called great in the kingdom of heaven. For I tell you, unless your righteousness exceeds that of the scribes and Pharisees, you will never enter the kingdom of heaven.

—Matthew 5:17–20

Key Terms

Theotokos

Christ

Prefigure

Incarnation

New Law

Sermon on the Mount

Theosis

Poverty

Compassion

Justification

Questions for Review

1. How does the angel Gabriel tell Mary she will become pregnant with Jesus?

2. What does the angel Gabriel mean when he calls Mary "full of grace"?

3. Name one prophecy from the Old Testament that Jesus fulfilled.

4. What was the purpose of the Incarnation?

5. What was Jesus's ultimate act of obedience to the Father and act of compassion for us?

Quiz

True/False

1. ____ Mary is the "God-bearer," or *Theosis*.
2. ____ Christ means "the anointed one."
3. ____ The Old Testament prefigures the coming of Christ.
4. ____ God sent his Son to earth for the salvation of humanity.

5. ____ Jesus could represent God because of his Divine Nature, but he could not represent humanity.

6. ____ The Law of the Gospel is contained clearly in the Prayer over Jerusalem.

7. ____ Another name for "divinization" is *Theotokos*.

8. ____ Jesus entered into the poverty of human nature and took on the life of the poor and suffering.

9. ____ Empathy means "suffering with."

10. ____ Through justification, we are freed from sin and made holy.

Questions for Discussion

1. What is one thing you learned about God the Father's love from Jesus's life on earth? Explain.

2. Our culture is fixated on wealth and material success, but Jesus lived on earth as a poor man. What does this tell us about wealth and poverty?

3. Jesus had great compassion for us. Who is someone you know that has had compassion for you? Describe what happened. What is one way you could have compassion for someone else?

Essay Questions / Further Study

1. Mary the Mother of God is revered in all ages and across the world. Research one Marian devotion in another part of the world. What aspect of Mary's life or character is celebrated, and how?

2. Using BibliaClerus.com or another Catholic Scripture commentary, read what the Church teaches about some of the Old Testament prophesies included in this chapter. How does Jesus clearly fulfil these prophecies?

3. Summarize the reasons why the Incarnation happened. Organize your points into a persuasive letter for a friend who does not believe that Jesus is the God who came to save all people.

4. Jesus became like us and shared particularly in the experience of suffering. Can you recount a time when the suffering of Jesus made a difference as you faced suffering?

5. In *Redemptor Hominis*, Pope St. John Paul II writes, "Human nature, by the very fact that it was assumed, not absorbed, in [Jesus] has been raised in us also to a dignity beyond compare." List the many ways that the Church seeks to uphold the dignity of the human person.

Part III

THE LIGHT OF SALVATION

Redemption Unfolds

The Beginning of Jesus's Public Ministry

Memory Verse

No temptation has overtaken you that is not common to man. God is faithful, and he will not let you be tempted beyond your strength, but with the temptation will also provide the way of escape, that you may be able to endure it.

—1 Corinthians 10:13

Key Terms

Baptism

John the Baptist

Disobedience

Temptation

Sign

Miracle

Questions for Review

1. In what way was each member of the Holy Trinity present at Jesus's baptism?

2. Why was it necessary for Jesus to be baptized, even though he was without sin?

3. What, ultimately, did Satan tempt Jesus to do?

4. How did Jesus combat these temptations?

5. What was the first public miracle Jesus performed?

Quiz

1. At Jesus's baptism in the Jordan River, _____ opened the heavens.
    A. God the Father
    B. God the Son
    C. God the Holy Spirit

2. At Jesus's baptism in the Jordan River, _____ appeared as a dove.
    A. God the Father
    B. God the Son
    C. God the Holy Spirit

3. Jesus's baptism foreshadows his:
    A. first miracle.
    B. death.
    C. priesthood.

4. Satan's tempting of Jesus to turn bread into stones and Jesus's answer refers to:
    A. Jesus's obedience to the Father.
    B. Jesus's refusal to use his power to prove his divinity
    C. Jesus's refusal to gain worldly power.

5. Satan's tempting of Jesus to throw himself off the temple and Jesus's answer refers to:
    A. Jesus's obedience to the Father.
    B. Jesus's refusal to use his power to prove his divinity.
    C. Jesus's refusal to gain worldly power.

6. Satan's offer of all the kingdoms of the world and Jesus's answer refers to:
    A. Jesus's obedience to the Father.
    B. Jesus's refusal to use his power to prove his divinity.
    C. Jesus's refusal to gain worldly power.

7. Jesus went through many trials, but he did not:
    A. face temptation.
    B. suffer.
    C. sin.

8. The first public miracle of Jesus foreshadowed:
    A. his death and resurrection.
    B. the Eucharist.
    C. the institution of the priesthood.

9. Jesus's first miracle was initiated by:
    A. his disciples.
    B. the bridegroom.
    C. his mother.

10. Mary's last recorded words in Scripture are:
    A. "Do whatever he tells you."
    B. "Let it be done unto me according to thy Word."
    C. "He must increase and I must decrease."

Questions for Discussion

1. What are three temptations you face regularly?

2. Has anything helped you overcome these temptations? If so, what? If not, what can you learn from the way Jesus handled temptation?

3. At Cana, Mary interceded for the bride and groom in their hour of need. Do you ever ask Mary to intercede for you? Why or why not?

Essay Topics / Further Study

1. Interview one of your parents or godparents about the day of your baptism. What details do they remember? How do you experience the effects of your baptism?

2. Create a dialogue between yourself and someone experiencing temptation. What advice would you offer that person? Be sure to use your knowledge of Jesus to encourage this person.

3. Find as many Scripture verses about doing God's will, choosing what is right, or anything else that will help you resist temptation. Keep the list someplace where you can reflect on it often.

4. Write a first-person account of the miracle at the wedding feast in Cana, from the perspective of one of his disciples who witnessed it. What did Jesus's miracle mean to you? Did you believe in him immediately?

5. Mary intercedes for us just as she did for the wedding feast at Cana. What are some ways that Mary intercedes for us? Give some examples from your life, or from the life of a family member or friend, or from the life of a saint where Mary's intercession was apparent.

The Height of Jesus's Ministry

Memory Verse

> So each of us shall give account of himself to God. Then let us no more pass judgment on one another, but rather decide never to put a stumbling block or hindrance in the way of a brother.

> —Romans 14:12–13

Key Terms

Kingdom of God

Conversion

Particular judgment

General judgment

Parables

The Church

Miracles

Binding and loosing

Keys of the kingdom

Transfiguration

Questions for Review

1. Who is called to enter the kingdom of God?

2. What form does the kingdom of God take on earth?

3. What is a parable? Give one example of a parable used by Jesus in the Gospels.

4. What was the ultimate purpose of Jesus's miracles?

5. To whom did Jesus give the authority to govern his kingdom on earth? Who possesses that authority today?

Quiz

1. The primary theme of Jesus's mission on earth was _____.

2. Jesus preached that _____ is called to enter the kingdom of God.

3. At the moment of death, in the _____, every individual will be judged according to their actions.

4. _____ are simple images or comparisons, often told through stories, that reveal some aspect of the kingdom.

5. Exorcisms, healings, resurrections, and control over nature are all types of Jesus's _____.

6. The signs Jesus performed testify that he comes from _____.

7. Jesus's mission wasn't to take away all earthy evils, but to free us from _____.

8. _____ refers to absolving sins, pronouncing doctrinal judgment, and making disciplinary decisions in the Church.

9. Only _____ received the keys of the kingdom.

10. Moses and Elijah, who appeared at the Transfiguration, represent the _____ _____.

Questions for Discussion

1. Why do you think the people of Jesus's day had a hard time recognizing him as the Messiah? What would you have expected the Messiah to be like? How was the reality different from those expectations?

2. Do you believe in miracles? Why or why not?

3. How can you proclaim the kingdom of God in your home, school, or community?

Essay Topics / Further Study

1. Compare the kingdom of God to a fictional kingdom. How do the "rules" differ?

2. The parables not only teach us about God's kingdom, they contain wisdom for living as a Christian. Choose one parable to study in depth. What are the different layers of meaning?

3. Choose one category of miracles (exorcisms, healings, resurrections, or control over nature) to examine. What are the specific examples of miracles that Jesus performed, and what does this category of miracles teach you about the Son of God?

4. Research a miracle that has been approved by the Catholic Church. What happened? What does this miracle teach us?

5. Discuss the ways in which the Transfiguration parallels Jesus's baptism. How did both prepare Jesus for the paschal mystery?

Jesus Institutes the Eucharist

Memory Verse

And he took bread, and when he had given thanks he broke it and gave it to them, saying, "This is my body which is given for you. Do this in remembrance of me." And likewise the cup after supper, saying, "This cup which is poured out for you is the new covenant in my blood."

—Luke 22:19–20

Key Terms

Passover

The Last Supper

Good Friday

Paschal mystery

Eucharist

New Covenant

Real Presence

Bread of Life Discourse

Mass

Luminous Mysteries

Questions for Review

1. What does the Passover supper recall?

2. In what ways did the Passover foreshadow the Eucharist?

3. What is the doctrine of the Real Presence?

4. How do we know, based on Scripture, that Jesus wasn't speaking metaphorically when he said that we must eat his flesh and drink his blood?

5. What elements of our own liturgy were present in the first days of the Church?

Quiz

True/False

1. ____ The Jewish Passover commemorates the annual atonement of sins.
2. ____ Jesus instituted the Eucharist and the priesthood of the New Covenant at the Resurrection.
3. ____ The Eucharist makes the paschal mystery present.
4. ____ The Catholic Church believes that the bread and wine consecrated at Mass are symbols of Jesus's Body and Blood.
5. ____ The scriptural basis for the doctrine of the Real Presence is found in the Bread of Life Discourse.
6. ____ Jesus spoke metaphorically about the need to eat his Body and drink his Blood.
7. ____ The Catechism calls the Eucharist and the Cross "stumbling blocks" because their mystery often leads people into disbelief.

8. ____ By the year 1000, the liturgy began to resemble the liturgy we celebrate today.

9. ____ St. Justin Martyr recounted that the early Church celebrated the liturgy with readings from the Old and New Testaments but did not include a homily on the readings.

10. ____ The major events of the public ministry of Jesus are remembered in the Luminous Mysteries of the Rosary.

Questions for Discussion

1. Why do you think it is important to receive the Eucharist at least every Sunday, and daily if possible?

2. How could simply spending time with the Eucharist, in prayer, help you grow closer to God?

3. What can make it difficult to believe that Jesus is really present in the Eucharist? Has anything made it easier for you to believe that he is really present?

Essay Topics / Further Study

1. Search online to find what Old Testament readings are used at the Jewish celebration of Passover. What readings are used at the Catholic Easter Vigil? Is there any overlap? Why is this significant?

2. Write a persuasive essay refuting one or more common objections to the Eucharist. As much as possible, try to use Scripture to make your argument.

3. Throughout the Church's history, there have been many Eucharistic miracles. Research one such miracle that has been officially approved by the Church. How does this miracle remind us that every celebration of the Eucharist is actually miraculous?

4. Write a report detailing where Catholic liturgies were celebrated in the early Church.

5. The Luminous Mysteries recall the major events of the public ministry of Jesus. List those mysteries and provide the Scripture references that they are derived from; then, explain the significance of each event.

Part IV

Christ Redeems Us Through His Paschal Mystery

THE PASSION AND DEATH OF JESUS

Memory Verse

Surely he has borne our griefs and carried our sorrows; yet we esteemed him stricken, smitten by God, and afflicted. But he was wounded for our transgressions, he was bruised for our iniquities; upon him was the chastisement that made us whole, and with his stripes we are healed. All we like sheep have gone astray; we have turned every one to his own way; and the LORD has laid on him the iniquity of us all.

—ISAIAH 53:4–6

Key Terms

Passion

The Agony in the Garden

The arrest and trial of Jesus

Judas

Pontius Pilate

Crucifixion

Suffering servant

Questions for Review

1. Who was responsible for Jesus's death?

2. What prophecy of Isaiah's did Jesus's passion and death fulfill?

3. On the cross, what did Jesus accomplish?

4. How does the concept of "ransom" help us understand Jesus's death?

5. How does the concept of "offering" or "sacrifice" help us understand Jesus's death?

Quiz

1. After the Last Supper, Jesus went to _____ to pray to the Father.
   A. the Temple of Jerusalem
   B. the upper room
   C. the garden of Gethsemane

2. _____ attempted to stop soldiers from arresting Jesus.
   A. Peter
   B. James
   C. John

3. Although he first offered to have Jesus pardoned, ultimately _____ had Jesus condemned to death.
   A. the High Priest
   B. Pontius Pilate
   C. Caesar

4. The Jewish people as a whole _____ responsible for the death of Jesus.
    A. are
    B. are not
    C. might be

5. Soldiers offered Jesus _____ as a painkiller during his passion.
    A. water and bitter herbs
    B. wine and bread
    C. wine and myrrh

6. _____ suffering servant prophecy is fulfilled by Jesus.
    A. Isaiah's
    B. Jeremiah's
    C. Ezekiel's

7. A _____ is the fee paid to free a person from captivity.
    A. debt
    B. recompense
    C. ransom

8. Although _____ was part of the Law of Moses, it couldn't take away sin.
    A. ritual cleansing
    B. animal sacrifice
    C. public confession

9. What God ultimately desired from his people was _____. Jesus modeled this for us.
    A. honesty
    B. prayer
    C. obedience

10. Jesus is the Lamb of God who fulfills the sacrifice of:
    A. Atonement.
    B. Passover.
    C. the Todah.

Questions for Discussion

1. Why is it easier to blame others for Jesus's death than it is to see how we, too, are responsible for it?

2. Jesus showed us how much he loves us by offering up his life for us. What does this teach you about love and greatness?

3. St. Paul teaches us that when we humbly accept our trials without complaint and unite them in prayer to Jesus's sufferings, they become a means of grace and redemption for others. What is one suffering you could "offer up" for someone else? Do you have someone specific in mind?

Essay Topics / Further Study

1. Pray the Stations of the Cross. Write a prayer for each of the stations.

2. Reread this chapter's assigned readings from the Gospel of Mark. Using this account, write your own summary of the passion of Christ. Write it like a story if you wish.

3. Explain in your own words the prophecy of the suffering servant of Isaiah and how Jesus fulfills the prophecy.

4. Write a personal reflection on how the suffering and death of Jesus on the cross has helped you face suffering in your own life.

5. How did Mary participate in the suffering of Jesus? What must it have been like to witness the death of her Son? How does Mary teach us to face painful experiences?

The Resurrection of Jesus

Memory Verse

|| O Lord, you have brought up my soul from Sheol, restored me to life from among those gone down to the Pit.

—Psalm 30:3

Key Terms

Hell

Sheol

Mary Magdalene

St. Paul

Resurrection

Paschal mystery

Eschatological

Questions for Review

1. What is *Sheol* and what did Jesus do there?

2. After his resurrection, to whom did Jesus first appear?

3. What is the significance of Jesus's resurrection?

4. What are the two aspects of the paschal mystery?

5. How do we participate in the paschal mystery?

Quiz

1. Before his resurrection, Jesus descended into the land of the dead, what was referred to as _____.

2. Jesus's resurrection was not a mere spiritual event, it was a _____ event.

3. _____ was the first to witness the Risen Jesus.

4. St. Paul says that Jesus appeared to more than _____ witnesses.

5. Jesus was not a _____: he ate with his disciples and let them touch his glorified body.

6. The Resurrection confirms the truth of Jesus's _____.

7. Jesus made _____ about his own resurrection.

8. The first aspect of the paschal mystery is Jesus's _____.

9. The second aspect of the paschal mystery is Jesus's _____.

10. We participate in the paschal mystery through _____.

Questions for Discussion

1. If we stay close to Jesus all our lives, after the final judgment, we, too, will have glorified bodies like him. To what aspect of having a glorified body are you most looking forward?

2. When it comes to death, of what are you most afraid? Does knowledge of Jesus and his resurrection lessen that fear? Why or why not?

3. How can you take better advantage of the graces offered to you in the sacraments?

Essay Topics / Further Study

1. Reflect on the selected reading from *Dives in Misericordia*. In what ways does the cross bear witness to God's mercy? Give examples from your own life or the lives of other Christians that make this reality clear.

2. Find sacred artwork that depicts the "Harrowing of Hell," or the liberation of souls from *sheol*. What Old Testament figures does the artwork depict? Why are they significant?

3. Construct a dialogue between yourself and a person who does not believe that the Resurrection was a historical event. What evidence can you use to persuade them of the historicity of the Resurrection? Is there more or less evidence than other widely accepted events in ancient history?

4. Do further research on the glorified body of the Resurrected Jesus. How does what we know about Jesus's glorified body inform us about what awaits our own bodies in eternity?

5. Make a list of the seven sacraments. For each sacrament, explain how we participate in the paschal mystery through it.

The Ascension of Jesus into Heaven

Memory Verse

When the day of Pentecost had come, they were all together in one place. And suddenly a sound came from heaven like the rush of a mighty wind, and it filled all the house where they were sitting. And there appeared to them tongues as of fire, distributed and resting on each one of them. And they were all filled with the Holy Spirit and began to speak in other tongues, as the Spirit gave them utterance.

—Acts 2:1–4

Key Terms

Ascension

Counselor

Pentecost

Intercession

Assumption

Questions for Review

1. How many days after the Resurrection did the Ascension occur?

2. On what feast day did the Holy Spirit descend upon the apostles?

3. What is the Holy Spirit's relationship to the sacraments?

4. Who is the Mother of the Church?

5. Upon whose power does the efficacy of Mary's prayers for us depend?

Quiz

True/False

1. ____ Jesus ascended into heaven fifty days after the Resurrection.
2. ____ Jesus now sits at the right hand of God as King and High Priest.
3. ____ When Jesus ascended into heaven, he abandoned us to this world for now.
4. ____ At the Ascension, the apostles were given the power to work miracles and the strength to witness to Jesus even to the point of suffering death.
5. ____ The Holy Spirit gives us the power to profess faith in Jesus.
6. ____ Jesus's death completed his earthly life.
7. ____ When Jesus returns in glory, the bodies of those in heaven will be raised up.
8. ____ Mary also shares in Jesus's glory, body and soul.
9. ____ In the Assumption, Jesus assumed Mary's soul into heaven.
10. ____ Mary's intercession is in complete unison with Jesus's intercession.

Questions for Discussion

1. Do you ever pray to the Holy Spirit? Why or why not?

2. What is one way you can follow Mary's example?

3. What are some of the things you ask your own mother to help you with? What are some of the things you could ask Mary to help you with?

Essay Topics / Further Study

1. Reflect on Acts 1:1–11. Writing in first person, prepare a letter from an apostle who witnessed Jesus's ascension. How would you feel after having spent the last forty days with the Resurrected Jesus?

2. What were the events that took place at Pentecost? Describe them. How was this like the birth of the Church? In what ways does the Church still experience the effects of Pentecost today? How do you experience the effects of Pentecost in your own life?

3. Orthodox Christians and some Eastern Rites of the Catholic Church have a particular devotion centered around the dormition of Mary. Although there are no biblical accounts, what traditions have been passed down regarding this event?

4. As Mother of the Church, Mary is an example for all Christians. Make a list of all the ways Mary teaches us what it means to be members of the Church.

5. In the selected reading from Pope Benedict XVI on the Ascension, we read how God makes himself close to us. In what ways have you experienced that Jesus is "with us always"? Name a time when you struggled to accept this truth.

Part V

THE PASCHAL MYSTERY AND THE LIFE OF THE BELIEVER

Jesus Dies for Our Sins and Was Raised for Our Justification

Memory Verse

For now we see in a mirror dimly, but then face to face. Now I know in part; then I shall understand fully, even as I have been fully understood. So faith, hope, love abide, these three; but the greatest of these is love.

—1 Corinthians 13:12–13

Key Terms

Theological virtues

Moral virtues

Particular judgment

Last judgment

Resurrection of the dead

Four last things

Purgatory

Venial sin

Questions for Review

1. Can we earn our own salvation and a place in heaven?

2. What are the three theological virtues? Give a short definition of each.

3. What is the particular judgment?

4. What is the last judgment?

5. What are the four last things? Give a short description of each.

Quiz

1. _____ is a rational acknowledgment that God is essentially mysterious.
   A. Philosophy
   B. Faith
   C. Theology

2. _____ forms the foundation upon which all commandments are based.
   A. Justice
   B. Mercy
   C. Love

3. The Our Father summarizes that _____ leads us to desire that God's name will be glorified, that his kingdom will come, his will shall be done, and more.
   A. prayer
   B. faith
   C. hope

4. At the _____, we will be held accountable for our actions.
   A. sacrament of Reconciliation
   B. particular judgment
   C. general judgment

5. At the end of time, the unjust will go forth to the:
   A. resurrection of judgment.
   B. land of Sheol.
   C. throne of God.

6. _____ is the separation of the soul from the body.
   A. Expiation
   B. Purgatory
   C. Death

7. In Jesus's time, many Jews believed in the:
   A. teaching of purgatory.
   B. resurrection of the dead.
   C. existence of venial sin.

8. The four last things does not include:
   A. purgatory.
   B. hell.
   C. death.

9. All earthly happiness points to:
   A. the Resurrection.
   B. heaven.
   C. freedom.

10. Purification of sin is much _____ on earth.
    A. easier
    B. harder
    C. more effective

Questions for Discussion

1. For each of the theological virtues, give one example of what the virtue looks like in action in your own life. In other words, give one concrete example of how you have demonstrated faith, hope, and charity.

2. Knowing that one day you will see Jesus face to face and he will judge all of your actions, what is one thing you have done that you are proud of? What is one thing you would want to do differently going forward?

3. The Church encourages us to think often about the four last things. Why do you think she does this?

Essay Topics / Further Study

1. The theological virtues help us live the divine life. Choose a character from literature or film that powerfully portrays one of the theological virtues. What does this character do that personifies the virtue? How does their example increase your understanding of the virtue?

2. Compile as many Scripture verses on the theological virtue of hope as you can find. Reflect on what hope means. What is life like without hope? How can you live with hope? How can you encourage others to be hopeful?

3. Many saints have written or spoken about praying for the souls in purgatory. Find examples of saints who prayed for the souls in purgatory. What advice do they give?

4. Love is the greatest of the theological virtues. Using the Catechism, Sacred Scripture, and other Catholic sources, compose an essay on what love is. Be sure to contrast the Catholic understanding of love with common depictions you have seen in the culture and in popular media.

5. There have long been debates in Catholic theology about hell. What does Jesus himself teach about hell? How do you see Jesus's words reflected in Church teaching?

We Are Called to Holiness

Memory Verse

> As obedient children, do not be conformed to the passions of your former ignorance, but as he who called you is holy, be holy yourselves in all your conduct; since it is written, "You shall be holy, for I am holy."
>
> —1 Peter 1:14–16

Key Terms

Holiness

Concupiscence

Mystical union

Conscience

Particular vocation

Confirmation

Penance

Matrimony

Holy Orders

Questions for Review

1. Who is called to holiness?

2. What virtue is at the heart of holiness?

3. What is our conscience?

4. How does our conscience help us in the pursuit of holiness?

5. How do the different sacraments help us in the pursuit of holiness?

Quiz

1. _____ is being conformed to Christ and sharing in the life of the Holy Trinity.

2. Through _____, God cleanses us from sin and makes us holy.

3. The tendency to sin is called _____.

4. Sharing in the mysteries of Christ leads us to a relationship called a _____.

5. The heart of holiness is _____.

6. Unlike animals, we have reason and _____ and are not driven solely by instinct.

7. _____ tells us that we must do what is good and avoid what is evil.

8. A way of life, such as religious life or marriage, is referred to as a
_____.

9. _____ to pursue holiness comes to us especially in the sacraments.

10. God helps us to grow in holiness through _____.

Questions for Discussion

1. When you think of holiness, what's the first thing that comes to mind? Why do you think this is?

2. Do you want to be holy? Why or why not?

3. What do you think being "holy" would be like? How would you be the same as you are today? How would you be different?

Essay Topics / Further Study

1. Write a reflection on the selected reading from *Lumen Gentium*. What does holiness look like in marriage? For priests and religious?

2. The saints are a tangible witness of holiness. Write a short biography of a saint from the twentieth century. How did they become holy?

3. Broadly speaking, what do you think prevents people from being holy? In what ways is a saint like an athlete? How are the characteristics of an athlete similar to those of a saint?

4. Explain what conscience is and isn't. What are some situations in which the well-formed conscience is particularly important?

5. Even if one does not feel called to the priesthood or religious life, it is good for all young people to consider these vocations. Choose a religious order to research. In what ways does this order live out the Gospel? What aspects of life in a religious order would be conducive to holiness? Would anything about religious life make it more difficult to pursue holiness?

Living as a Disciple of Jesus

Memory Verse

|| Return to the Lord, your God, for he is gracious and merciful, slow to anger, and abounding in steadfast love, and repents of evil.

—Joel 2:13

Key Terms

Conversion

Ongoing conversion

Discipleship

Worship

Evangelical counsels

Poverty

Chastity

Obedience

Questions for Review

1. To whom is the call of conversion addressed?

2. What does "ongoing conversion" mean?

3. What are three things that can help us in the process of ongoing conversion?

4. What are the evangelical counsels?

5. What are two ways of loving our neighbor modeled for us by Jesus?

Quiz

True/False

1. ____ Jesus's preaching began with a call to seek justice for the poor.
2. ____ Both the unbaptized and baptized are called to conversion.
3. ____ The closer we grow to Jesus, the more we can see our own need for ongoing conversion.
4. ____ Poverty is at the center of discipleship.
5. ____ God deserves our love and worship as a matter of justice.
6. ____ We love and worship God through the sacraments.
7. ____ The model and best teacher of prayer is John the Baptist.
8. ____ Married people commit to living the evangelical counsels.
9. ____ Jesus tells us to pray for our enemies, but we are not obligated to love them.
10. ____ Loving our neighbor means looking after not only their physical but also their spiritual needs.

Questions for Discussion

1. What is one practical thing you could do to show your love for God more?

2. What is one practical thing you could do to show your love for your family more?

3. Are you comfortable sharing your faith with others? Why or why not? What is one practical thing you could do to help others know about God's love?

Essay Topics / Further Study

1. In this chapter's selected reading from *Spe Salvi*, Pope Benedict writes about the remarkable conversion of St. Augustine. Write a short biography detailing the conversion story of someone you know. Or pick a saint and describe their conversion. Be sure to detail what life is like before and after one's conversion.

2. Find an example of conversion that occurs in the New Testament. Explain what happened. If Scripture does not give details, reflect on what you think happened after the person's initial conversion.

3. Write out your personal goals to help facilitate your own ongoing conversion. What will you include in your plan to ensure that you are maturing in your faith? Which resources and sacraments will you make us of? Is there someone who can hold you accountable?

4. Choose one of the evangelical counsels to research further. What can you find in Church teaching about this virtue? What impact can it have in the life of the person who commits to it?

5. Jesus teaches us that "our neighbor" is everyone in need of compassion, especially those who are ignored or cast aside by society—such as the poor, the elderly, the sick, the unborn, the marginalized, those with special needs, and those who struggle with particular sins. With this understanding in mind, make a list with as many concrete ways of loving your neighbor that you can think of.

Part VI

PRAYER IN THE LIFE OF A BELIEVER

God Calls Every Individual to Prayer

Memory Verse

Rejoice always, pray constantly, give thanks in all circumstances; for this is the will of God in Christ Jesus for you.

—1 Thessalonians 5:16–18

Key Terms

Prayer

St. Augustine

St. John Damascus

Private revelation

Divine revelation

Questions for Review

1. What is prayer?

2. How did God publicly speak to humanity?

3. Why are we able to have a personal relationship with God?

4. How can we hear God's voice in prayer?

5. How does prayer put us in relation with all three members of the Trinity?

Quiz

1. _____ said, "You have made us for yourself, O Lord, and our hearts are restless until they rest in you."
   A. Jesus
   B. St. Thomas Aquinas
   C. St. Augustine

2. The Catechism says that it is the _____ that prays.
   A. heart
   B. mind
   C. soul

3. _____ described prayer as "the raising of one's mind and heart to God."
   A. St. John the Apostle
   B. St. John of Damascus
   C. St. John Cantius

4. The process of prayer can be described as:
   A. "falling in love."
   B. "meditation."
   C. "communication."

5. _____ is a necessary part of fulfilling the first and greatest commandment.
   A. Justice
   B. Conversion
   C. Prayer

6. God _____ reveals himself to people through private revelations or spiritual experiences.
   A. always
   B. sometimes
   C. never

7. We primarily hear God through:
   A. divine revelation.
   B. private revelation.
   C. other people.

8. We can have a relationship with God because Jesus _____ us to him.
   A. introduces
   B. converts
   C. reconciles

9. It is _____ who moves us to prayer.
   A. God the Father
   B. Jesus
   C. the Holy Spirit

10. Jesus is truly present in:
    A. the Church.
    B. an audible voice.
    C. the apostles' teaching.

Questions for Discussion

1. Do you pray regularly? Why or why not?

2. Is it easy or difficult for you to share your feelings with God? Explain.

3. What are some of the things you talk to your family and friends about? Do you talk to God about those things as well? Why or why not?

Essay Topics / Further Study

1. A number of saints, popes, and spiritual writers have written movingly about prayer. Ask your parish priest or another Catholic you look up to for a recommended book on prayer. After reading, write a review of the book.

2. The Catechism has a whole section on prayer. Read as much as you can. What insights can you gain from Church teaching on prayer?

3. Write a letter to a friend about a personal experience you have had with prayer.

4. Most people will never experience private revelation. However, the Church has approved of a number of private revelations. Research an example of private revelation that was approved by the Church. What can you learn from this example?

5. Using Scripture, show when and how Jesus taught us followers how to pray.

SOURCES, GUIDES, AND EXPRESSIONS OF PRAYER

Memory Verse

|| Rejoice in your hope, be patient in tribulation, be constant in prayer.

—ROMANS 12:12

Key Terms

Adam and Eve

Abraham

Moses

David

Solomon

The Temple

Elijah

Psalms

Liturgy of the Hours

The Rosary

The Angelus

Lectio Divina

Vocal prayer

Mental prayer

Meditation

Contemplation

Questions for Review

1. Who are two exemplary models of prayer in the Old Testament? What is one lesson we can learn from each?

2. What book of the Bible is filled with prayerful songs that we should continue to pray today?

3. Name two important lessons Jesus taught us about prayer.

4. What is an ancient method of praying using Scripture? Describe it.

5. What are the four different expressions of prayer?

Quiz

1. As a mediator between God and Israel, _____ is a type of Jesus, the one mediator between God and man.

2. _____ wanted to build a permanent place of worship in Jerusalem, but God wouldn't allow it.

3. The prophet _____ modeled fidelity to God, believing that he would honor his prayers.

4. The _____ were hymns used by Israel in their synagogues at the celebration of the great feasts in Jerusalem.

5. Jesus taught us to approach God in prayer as a _____.

6. _____ is a form of prayer prayed daily by priests, deacons, and religious.

7. _____ is a short prayer that meditates on a series of events in the lives of Jesus and Mary in Scripture.

8. Reading Scripture in a meditative, prayerful way is an ancient practice called _____.

9. _____ acknowledges that we pray with our whole being—body and soul.

10. _____ is a prayer that goes beyond words to let us simply be in God's presence for a time.

Questions for Discussion

1. Of all the Old Testament figures named here, which one teaches you a lesson about prayer that you think you need right now? Explain.

2. How could you carve out more time in your day to be alone with God? Is there a particular place you like to pray or would like to go to pray?

3. Do you have a favorite prayer? If so, what is it and what about it do you like?

Essay Topics / Further Study

1. In this chapter's selected reading from *Verbum Domini*, Pope Benedict XVI remarks that "the process of *lectio divina* is not concluded until it arrives at action (*actio*), which moves the believer to make his or her life a gift for others in charity." Choose a passage of Scripture to practice *lectio divina*. Journal about the process, and write a goal for acting upon what you have learned through your meditation.

2. Find an example from either the Old or New Testament, not listed in this chapter, of prayer. What expression of prayer is exemplified? What does this passage teach us about the experience of prayer? About God?

3. Using BibliaClerus.org or another Catholic Scripture commentary, choose a Psalm to study. How does the commentary help you understand this Psalm better? Find as much information about this Psalm as you can.

4. Using a missal, find as many uses of Scripture in the Mass as you can. Think beyond the Liturgy of the Word.

5. Imagine that a non-Catholic friend has asked you what you believe about prayer. With the help of Scripture, and particularly the New Testament, explain the importance of prayer. Explain the difference between public and private prayer and the example set by Christ.

FORMS AND HABITS OF PRAYER

Memory Verse

|| O come, let us worship and bow down, let us kneel before the LORD, our Maker!

—PSALM 95:6

Key Terms

Blessing

Adoration

Petition

Intercession

Thanksgiving

Praise

Consolation

Spiritual dryness

Presumption

Acedia

The Lord's Prayer

Questions for Review

1. What are the six forms of prayer?

2. What is an example of each form of prayer?

3. What difficulties can arise in prayer?

4. How do we overcome these difficulties?

5. What prayer is considered a "catechism" on prayer? Explain.

Quiz

True/False

1. ____ We bless God in prayer.
2. ____ The Catechism calls intercession "the first act of the virtue of religion."
3. ____ The first prayer of petition at Mass is the Prayers of the Faithful.
4. ____ The word *Eucharist* means "give thanks."
5. ____ Praise embraces the other forms of prayer.
6. ____ Feelings of peace, contentment, or joy in prayer are known as exultation.
7. ____ Spiritual dryness is a sign that God is displeased with us.
8. ____ Presumption is an attitude that leads us to only turn to God as a last resort.
9. ____ Spiritual depression that comes from being lax in prayer is called discouragement.
10. ____ The Nicene Creed is referred to as a brief catechism on prayer.

Questions for Discussion

1. Of the six forms of prayer, which forms do you most commonly use? Which don't you use? How could using more forms of prayer deepen your relationship with God?

2. What are some of your most common distractions in prayer? What does this say about what you are attached to and prioritize in life?

3. Is it difficult for you to trust God and persist in prayer? Why or why not?

Essay Topics / Further Study

1. Choose one of the six forms of prayer to study deeply. Write a descriptive essay about this form. Use the Catechism, the Bible, and the writings of the saints and popes for your sources.

2. What Old and New Testament examples of Adoration can you find? Why is Adoration so important?

3. Many saints have experienced and written about spiritual dryness. One such saint was St. Teresa of Calcutta. Research Mother Teresa's experience. With this understanding, what does her dedication to daily prayer and missionary work mean? What can you learn from her witness?

4. Using the method of *lectio divina* that you learned in the previous chapter, pray the Lord's Prayer. Write a short reflection on each of the statements within the prayer.

5. Reflect on all that you have learned about prayer. Now construct a dialogue between two friends: one who sees and experiences the value of prayer in their own life and one who does not think that prayer is necessary. What evidence from Church teaching, Scripture, and the witness of Christian disciples can you use to convince the unbeliever?

Final Exam

_____ / 100

Matching

2 points each

A. Angels
B. Prayer
C. Contemplation
D. Logos
E. Love
F. *Lectio Divina*
G. Original justice
H. Paschal mystery
I. Faith
J. Satan
K. Tower of Babel
L. Sheol
M. Christ
N. Protoevangelium
O. Ransom
P. Original sin
Q. Covenant
R. Rainbow
S. Concupiscence
T. Parables
U. The Tree of the Knowledge of Good and Evil
V. The Decalogue
W. *Theotokos*
X. *Theosis*
Y. Particular judgment

_____ 1. Fee paid to free a person from captivity
_____ 2. The Ten Commandments
_____ 3. God's delivery of all mankind from sin and death through the blood of Jesus on the cross
_____ 4. Means logic
_____ 5. The offering of our hearts and minds to God
_____ 6. The "God-bearer"
_____ 7. The sin of our first parents
_____ 8. Reading Scripture in a meditative, prayerful way is an ancient practice called
_____ 9. A fallen angel created by God who at some point sinned and radically and permanently rejected God
_____ 10. Purely spiritual, nonmaterial beings
_____ 11. The anointed one
_____ 12. The state human beings were created in while in the Garden of Eden, in perfect harmony
_____ 13. A symbol of the boundaries placed on mankind
_____ 14. A symbol of the covenant God made with Noah
_____ 15. A manifestation of pride
_____ 16. Means "divinization"
_____ 17. A rational acknowledgment that God is essentially mysterious
_____ 18. The dwelling place of the dead
_____ 19. A prayer that goes beyond words to let us simply be in God's presence for a time
_____ 20. The "first gospel"
_____ 21. The judgment of each person at their death
_____ 22. A solemn, family-making commitments
_____ 23. An inclination to sin
_____ 24. Simple images or comparisons, often told through stories
_____ 25. The heart of holiness

Short Answer

5 Points Each

1. What questions does the creation account in Genesis seek to answer? What questions does it not seek to answer?

2. What does it mean for man to be a steward of creation?

3. Why does the Church call Jesus the "New Adam" and Mary the "New Eve"?

4. Name two ways Baptism was prefigured in the Old Covenant.

5. What does the angel Gabriel mean when he calls Mary "full of grace"?

6. What is a parable? Give one example of a parable used by Jesus in the Gospels.

7. What are the four last things? Give a short description of each.

8. How do we know, based on Scripture, that Jesus wasn't speaking metaphorically when he said that we must eat his flesh and drink his blood?

9. What are the three theological virtues? Give a short definition of each.

10. What does "ongoing conversion" mean?

Answer Key

Part I: Chapter 1 — The Creation of the World and Our First Parents

Questions for Review

1. What questions does the creation account in Genesis seek to answer? What questions does it not seek to answer?

The creation account in Genesis seeks to answer questions about the religious truth of creation and the religious truth about man. It does not seek to answer questions about science or history.

2. What do we mean when we say God is the creator of all things "visible and invisible"?

When we say God is creator of all things "visible and invisible," we mean that God created both the material world and spiritual realities.

3. Through whom did God create the world?

God created the world through his Son, the "Word" of God.

4. Who created God?

No one created God. He is uncreated.

5. What are angels?

Angels are purely spiritual, nonmaterial beings who serve as the servants and messengers of God.

Quiz

1. B
2. B
3. C
4. C
5. A
6. B
7. A
8. C
9. B
10. A

Part I: Chapter 2—Human Beings: The Summit of Creation

Questions for Review

1. What does it mean for man to be a steward of creation?

Being a steward of creation means exercising dominion over the world, acting as caretakers so that others can enjoy the fruits of creation and so that we can offer all the goods of creation back to God in thanksgiving.

2. What sets the human person apart from all the other creatures of the earth?

The human person, unlike all other creatures on earth, is made in the image and likeness of God and has a spiritual and immortal soul that can know God and share in his life.

3. How do married persons and families image God?

Married persons reflect God because their unity makes them "one flesh," and when they make a total gift of themselves and create a third person, they reflect the Trinity: a communion of persons united in love that is generous and life giving.

4. A human person is a perfect union of what two things?

A human person is a perfect union of body and soul.

5. What do we call the original state of harmony that existed in the Garden?

We call the original state of harmony that existed in the Garden "original justice."

Quiz

1. human beings
2. dominion
3. God
4. communion of persons
5. Chastity
6. soul
7. material/physical and spiritual
8. the person
9. harmony
10. original justice

Part I: Chapter 3—The Fall from Grace: Original Sin

Questions for Review

1. Who is Satan?

Satan is a fallen angel created by God who at some point sinned and radically and permanently rejected God.

2. What did Satan promise Adam and Eve?

Satan promised Adam and Eve that they would not die if they ate from the tree of knowledge of good and evil but that their eyes would be opened and they would become like God.

3. What did Adam and Eve lose when they disobeyed God?

When Adam and Eve disobeyed God they lost original holiness and justice, as well as sanctifying grace and immortality.

4. What do we call the sin of our first parents and the fallen state of human nature inherited from them?

The sin of our first parents and the fallen state of human nature we inherited from them is called original sin.

5. After announcing their punishment for sin, what good news does God give Adam and Eve?

After announcing their punishment for sin, the good news God gives Adam and Eve is that he will send a savior to rescue fallen humanity.

Quiz

1. True
2. False; permanently rejected God
3. False; They were free from sin, suffering, and death
4. True
5. True
6. True
7. False; It is the loss of sanctifying grace
8. True
9. False; We are born with original sin
10. False; concupiscence

Part II: Chapter 1 — The First Prophecy of the Messiah

Questions for Review

1. What is the "protoevangelium"?

The "protoevangelium" or "first gospel" is the first, partial unveiling of God's plan to send a savior to mankind.

2. Why does the Church call Jesus the "New Adam"?

The Church calls Jesus the "New Adam" because, just as sin came into the world through one man, Adam, so salvation comes through the obedience of one man, Jesus.

3. Why does the Church call Mary the "New Eve"?

The Church calls Mary the "New Eve" because, similar to how Adam's sin occurred through the help of Eve, Jesus's work of salvation occurs with the cooperation of Mary.

4. What is the first way we see sin escalate after the fall of Adam and Eve?

The first way we see sin escalate after the fall of Adam and Eve is through the jealousy, lying, lack of concern for one's neighbor, and murder committed by Cain.

5. What does the Tower of Babel symbolize?

The Tower of Babel symbolizes the sin of pride.

Quiz

1. C
2. C
3. C
4. A
5. C
6. B
7. A
8. C
9. C
10. A

Part II: Chapter 2—Longing for the Fulfillment of the Promise

Questions for Review

1. What are covenants?

Covenants are solemn, family-making commitments.

2. What does a sacrifice offered to God express?

A sacrifice offered to God expresses the fact that everything we have belongs to God and that we depend upon him and trust in him rather than in our own power and wealth.

3. Name three figures from the Old Testament with whom God made covenants.

God made covenants with Noah, Abraham, and Moses.

4. What was the role of the Judges in ancient Israel?

The role of the Judges was to remind God's people of their covenant with him and then to lead them to victory over their enemies.

5. Name two ways Baptism was prefigured in the Old Covenant.

Possible Answers: Baptism was prefigured in the Old Covenant in the Flood, circumcision, and the deliverance of God's people through the parting of the Red Sea.

Quiz

1. Covenants
2. Sacrifice
3. rainbow
4. circumcision
5. The Decalogue or The Ten Commandments
6. Types
7. Passover
8. Paschal Mystery
9. Judges
10. Prophets

Part II: Chapter 3—The Promise Fulfilled

Questions for Review

1. How does the angel Gabriel tell Mary she will become pregnant with Jesus?

The angel Gabriel tells Mary she will conceive by the power of the Holy Spirit and, therefore, her Child will be the Son of God.

2. What does the angel Gabriel mean when he calls Mary "full of grace"?

When the angel Gabriel calls Mary "full of grace," he means that she is free from sin so that she could bring Jesus into the world.

3. Name one prophecy from the Old Testament that Jesus fulfilled.

Possible answers: "A virgin shall conceive and bear a son." / "Out of Egypt have I called my son." / "The land of Zeb'ulun and the land of Naph'tali . . . the people who sat in darkness have seen a great light." / "He took our infirmities and bore our diseases." / "He will not wrangle or cry aloud." / "I will open my mouth in parables." / "Behold, your king is coming to you, humble, and mounted on a donkey." / "He has blinded their eyes and hardened their heart." / "He who ate my bread has lifted his heel against me."

4. What was the purpose of the Incarnation?

The purpose of the Incarnation was the salvation of humanity.

5. What was Jesus's ultimate act of obedience to the Father and act of compassion for us?

Jesus's ultimate act of obedience to the Father and act of compassion for us was offering his life on the cross.

Quiz

1. False: *Theotokos*
2. True
3. True
4. True
5. False: Because of his human nature, Jesus could also represent all of humanity
6. False: The Sermon on the Mount
7. False: *Theosis*
8. True
9. False: Compassion
10. True

Part III: Chapter 1—The Beginning of Jesus's Public Ministry

Questions for Review

1. In what way was each member of the Holy Trinity present at Jesus's baptism?

At Jesus's baptism, Jesus was present in the river, God the Father opened the heavens and revealed the divine Personhood of Jesus, and the Holy Spirit appeared as a dove, revealing that Jesus is the Messiah or Christ.

2. Why was it necessary for Jesus to be baptized, even though he was without sin?

Though he was without sin, Jesus was baptized to "fulfil all righteousness," submitting himself entirely to the Father's will, allowing himself to be numbered among sinners and show the way to salvation.

3. What, ultimately, did Satan tempt Jesus to do?

Ultimately, Satan tempted Jesus to use his power for himself: to satisfy his desires, to gain wealth and power, and to enjoy the glory and adoration of the world.

4. How did Jesus combat these temptations?

Jesus combated the temptations of Satan by quoting Scripture and remaining obedient to his Father in all things.

5. What was the first public miracle Jesus performed?

The first public miracle Jesus performed was turning water to wine at the wedding feast at Cana.

Quiz

1. A
2. C
3. B
4. A
5. B
6. C
7. C
8. B
9. C
10. A

Part III: Chapter 2—The Height of Jesus's Ministry

Questions for Review

1. Who is called to enter the kingdom of God?

Everyone is called to enter the kingdom of God.

2. What form does the kingdom of God take on earth?

The form the kingdom of God takes on earth is the Church.

3. What is a parable? Give one example of a parable used by Jesus in the Gospels.

A parable is a simple image or comparison, often told through a story, that reveals some aspect of the kingdom. Examples include the parable of the mustard seed, the parable of the

leaven, the parable of the weed among the weeds, the parable of the hidden treasure, the parable of the pearl of great price, and the parable of the sower.

4. What was the ultimate purpose of Jesus's miracles?

The ultimate purpose of Jesus's miracles was to show that he came from the Father and to invite people to believe in him, or to strengthen the faith of those who already believe.

5. To whom did Jesus give the authority to govern his kingdom on earth? Who possesses that authority today?

Jesus gave Peter the authority to govern his kingdom on earth. Today, that authority is possessed by the pope.

Quiz

1. The Kingdom of God
2. everyone
3. Particular Judgment
4. Parables
5. miracles
6. the Father
7. slavery to sin or sin
8. Binding and loosing
9. Peter
10. Law and the Prophets

Part III: Chapter 3—Jesus Institutes the Eucharist

Questions for Review

1. What does the Passover supper recall?

The Passover supper recalls God's deliverance of the Israelites from slavery and death.

2. In what ways did the Passover foreshadow the Eucharist?

The Passover foreshadowed the Eucharist because in commemorating the Israelites delivery from slavery and death, the Eucharist commemorates Jesus's delivery of all people from death and slavery to sin. The Passover meal foreshadowed the Eucharistic bread and wine.

3. What is the doctrine of the Real Presence?

The doctrine of the Real Presence is the belief that the consecrated bread and wine of the Eucharist are the true Body and Blood of Jesus, who is substantially present in them.

4. How do we know, based on Scripture, that Jesus wasn't speaking metaphorically when he said that we must eat his flesh and drink his blood?

We know, based on Scripture, that Jesus wasn't speaking metaphorically when he said that we must eat his flesh and drink his blood because in John 3:3–7 when Nicodemus objected to Jesus saying that one must be "born again," Jesus clarified his symbolic meaning from the literal meaning of his words. He does not do so anywhere in John 6, and in fact, "doubles down" on his words, repeating them more emphatically.

5. What elements of our own liturgy were present in the first days of the Church?

The elements of our own liturgy that were present in the first days of the Church are readings from the Old and New Testaments, a homily on the readings, intercessory prayers, the exchange of the sign of peace, the Eucharistic Prayer, the distribution of consecrated bread and wine, and sending the consecrated bread to believers who aren't present at the liturgy.

Quiz

1. False: commemorates the freeing of Israelite slaves from Egypt
2. False: At the Last Supper
3. True
4. False: The Church holds that Jesus's Body and Blood are truly present in the consecrated bread and wine
5. True
6. False: Jesus spoke *literally* about the need to eat his Body and drink his Blood
7. True
8. False: By the year AD 155, or in the early Church
9. False: the early Church did include a homily on the readings
10. True

Part IV: Chapter 1 — The Passion and Death of Jesus

Questions for Review

1. Who was responsible for Jesus's death?

All sinners are responsible for the death of Jesus.

2. What prophecy of Isaiah's did Jesus's passion and death fulfill?

Jesus's passion and death fulfilled Isaiah's prophecy about the Suffering Servant.

3. On the cross, what did Jesus accomplish?

On the cross, Jesus accomplished our salvation. Jesus bore the consequence of sin on the cross, purchasing for us freedom with his Blood.

4. How does the concept of "ransom" help us understand Jesus's death?

A "ransom" is the price paid to free someone from captivity. Jesus paid the price of our sin through his death. Additionally, the verb "to ransom" has a meaning similar to "to redeem."

5. How does the concept of "offering" or "sacrifice" help us understand Jesus's death?

Throughout history, human beings have made "offerings" or "sacrifices" to God to atone for sin. But none were able to fully do this. In this light, we can better understand that Jesus's death is the only offering or sacrifice that can actually take away our sins.

Quiz

1. C
2. A
3. B
4. B
5. C
6. A
7. C
8. B
9. C
10. B

Part IV: Chapter 2—The Resurrection of Jesus

Questions for Review

1. What is *sheol* and what did Jesus do there?

***Sheol* refers to the dwelling place of the dead. Jesus descended into hell, or *sheol*, to free the souls there from death.**

2. After his resurrection, to whom did Jesus first appear?

After his resurrection, Jesus first appeared to Mary Magdalene and the holy women who had come to anoint his body.

3. What is the significance of Jesus's resurrection?

The significance of Jesus's resurrection is that it confirms the truth of Jesus's divinity and it confirms that everything he did and taught was done with divine authority. It also fulfills the promises made in the Old Testament and Jesus's own predictions. Finally, the Resurrection was the second aspect of the paschal mystery, which opens the way to a new life for us.

4. What are the two aspects of the paschal mystery?

The two aspects of the paschal mystery are Jesus's suffering and death on the cross and the Resurrection.

5. How do we participate in the paschal mystery?

We participate in the paschal mystery through the sacraments, above all through the Eucharist.

Quiz

1. Sheol
2. historical
3. Mary Magdalene
4. 500
5. ghost
6. divinity
7. promises or predictions
8. suffering and death
9. Resurrection
10. the sacraments or the Eucharist

Part IV: Chapter 3 — The Ascension of Jesus into Heaven

Questions for Review

1. How many days after the Resurrection did the Ascension occur?

The Ascension occurred forty days after the Resurrection.

2. On what feast day did the Holy Spirit descend upon the apostles?

The Holy Spirit descended upon the apostles on the feast of Pentecost.

3. What is the Holy Spirit's relationship to the sacraments?

It is the Holy Spirit who makes Jesus present in the sacraments.

4. Who is the Mother of the Church?

Mary is the Mother of the Church

5. Upon whose power does the efficacy of Mary's prayers for us depend?

The efficacy of Mary's prayers for us depends on the power of Jesus.

Quiz

1. False: forty days
2. True
3. False: Jesus promised to remain with us always
4. False: at Pentecost
5. True
6. False: His ascension
7. True
8. True
9. False: Mary was assumed body and soul into heaven
10. False: Mary's intercession is entirely *dependent* on Jesus

Part V: Chapter 1—Jesus Dies for Our Sins and was Raised for Our Justification

Questions for Review

1. Can we earn our own salvation and a place in heaven?

We cannot earn our own salvation or a place in heaven. Salvation is a gift, and heaven is a continuation of our new life in Christ that God gives us now.

2. What are the three theological virtues? Give a short definition of each.

The three theological virtues are faith, hope, and love (or charity). Faith is the theological virtue by which we believe in God, in all that he has said and revealed to us, and in all that his Church proposes for our belief. Hope is the theological virtue by which we desire the kingdom of heaven and eternal life as our happiness, placing our trust in Christ's promises and relying not on our own strength but on the help of the grace of the Holy Spirit. Charity is the theological virtue by which we love God above all things for his own sake and our neighbor as ourselves for the love of God.

3. What is the particular judgment?

The particular judgment occurs at the moment of death. We will be judged when we die according to our works and our acceptance or refusal of grace.

4. What is the last judgment?

The last judgment will occur at the end of time. Our souls will be reunited with our bodies and the just will experience the resurrection of life. The unjust will go forth to the resurrection of judgment.

5.What are the four last things? Give a short description of each.

Death, judgment, heaven, and hell are the four last things. Death is the separation of the soul from the body. Judgment is how we will give an account to God for how we've responded to

his grace. Heaven is a communion of life and love with the Holy Trinity, Mary, and all the saints and angels. Heaven is the fulfillment of all our desires and the state of supreme happiness. Hell is the separation from God caused by our own free choice to reject God's mercy.

Quiz

1. B
2. C
3. C
4. B
5. A
6. C
7. B
8. A
9. B
10. A

Part V: Chapter 2—We Are Called to Holiness

Questions for Review

1. Who is called to holiness?

All Christians are called to holiness.

2. What virtue is at the heart of holiness?

The theological virtue of charity (or love) is at the heart of holiness.

3. What is our conscience?

Conscience is a judgment of reason whereby the human person recognizes the moral quality of a concrete act that he is going to perform, is in the process of performing, or has already completed.

4. How does our conscience help us in the pursuit of holiness?

Our conscience helps us in the pursuit of holiness by strengthening us to choose what is right over what is wrong.

5. How do the different sacraments help us in the pursuit of holiness?

The sacraments help us in the pursuit of holiness by giving us the graces we need to grow closer to God and practice habitual virtue.

Quiz

1. Holiness
2. Baptism
3. concupiscence
4. mystical union
5. charity or love
6. free will
7. Conscience
8. particular vocation
9. Grace
10. Possible Answers: the teaching and guidance of our pope, bishops, and priests/ the support of our fellow believers/ through the example and prayers of the saints.

Part V: Chapter 3—Living as a Disciple of Jesus

Questions for Review

1. To whom is the call of conversion addressed?

The call to conversion is addressed, in part, to those who don't know Jesus and his Gospel. But it is also addressed to all who are baptized.

2. What does "ongoing conversion" mean?

"Ongoing conversion" means that we don't just choose to follow Christ for once and for all: throughout our lives, we must continue to mature and grow in our faith.

3. What are three things that can help us in the process of ongoing conversion?

Three things that can help us in the process of ongoing conversion are studying the Church's teachings, reading the lives of the saints, and attending retreats. Other possible answers include listening to talks about the faith and persisting in prayer and worship.

4. What are the evangelical counsels?

The evangelical counsels are poverty, chastity, and obedience. These virtues enable those who live consecrated life to remain faithful to their vows.

5. What are two ways of loving our neighbor modeled for us by Jesus?

Two ways of loving our neighbor modeled for us by Jesus are loving people outside of our family and loving our enemies. (Other answer: Laying down our lives for our friends, sharing what we have with our neighbors.)

Quiz

1. False; a call to conversion
2. True
3. True
4. False; Love is at the center of discipleship
5. True
6. True
7. False; Jesus
8. False; Consecrated people
9. False; Jesus tells us to pray for and to love our enemies
10. True

Part VI: Chapter 1—God Calls Every Individual to Prayer

Questions for Review

1. What is prayer?

Prayer is offering of our minds and hearts to God.

2. How did God publicly speak to humanity?

God has spoken through divine Revelation—in Scripture and through Tradition.

3. Why are we able to have a personal relationship with God?

We are able to have a personal relationship with God because he sent Jesus to reconcile us to him.

4. How can we hear God's voice in prayer?

We can hear God's voice in prayer through ordinary experience, in the blessings he does or doesn't give us, in the movements of our hearts, or in the words of the people he puts in our lives.

5. How does prayer put us in relation with all three members of the Trinity?

The prayer of the Church is addressed to God the Father; the Holy Spirit moves us to prayer; and Jesus is our mediator to God the Father in prayer.

Quiz

1. C
2. A
3. B
4. A
5. C

6. B
7. A
8. C
9. C
10. A

Part VI: Chapter 2—Sources, Guides, and Expressions of Prayer

Questions for Review

1. Who are two exemplary models of prayer in the Old Testament? What is one lesson we can learn from each?

Possible answers: Adam and Eve, Abraham, Moses, David, and Elijah. See text for lessons learned from each.

2. What book of the Bible is filled with prayerful songs that we should continue to pray today?

The book of the Bible filled with prayerful songs that we should continue to pray today is the Psalms.

3. Name two important lessons Jesus taught us about prayer.

Two important lessons Jesus taught us about prayer are the need to take time to develop our relationship with God alone and that we should address God as Father. (Other answers: We should use prayer to help us accept God's will, especially in times of suffering, and that a life lived for God is a life of prayer.)

4. What is an ancient method of praying using Scripture? Describe it.

An ancient method of praying using Scripture is *Lectio Divina*. It involves reading through the Scriptures or other spiritual writings prayerfully as a way to engage in prayer.

5. What are the four different expressions of prayer?

The four different expressions of prayer are vocal prayer, mental prayer, meditation, and contemplation.

Quiz

1. Moses
2. David
3. Elijah
4. Psalms
5. Father
6. The Liturgy of the Hours

7. The Angelus
8. *Lectio Divina*
9. Vocal prayer
10. Contemplation

Part VI: Chapter 3—Forms and Habits of Prayer

Questions for Review

1. What are the six forms of prayer?

The six forms of prayer are blessing, adoration, petition, intercession, thanksgiving, and praise.

2. What is an example of each form of prayer?

Blessing: The Offertory, the Eucharistic Prayer

Adoration: Adoring God our Creator

Petition: The Penitential Rite

Intercession: The Prayers of the Faithful

Thanksgiving: The Eucharist

Praise: The Gloria

3. What difficulties can arise in prayer?

Difficulties that can arise in prayer include distraction, spiritual dryness, and temptations.

4. How do we overcome these difficulties?

To overcome difficulties that can arise in prayer, we must trust in God.

5. What prayer is considered a "catechism" on prayer? Explain.

The Our Father is considered a "catechism" on prayer because it teaches us about the most central elements of prayer: thanksgiving, praise, and repentance.

Quiz

1. True
2. False; Adoration
3. False; The Penitential Rite
4. True
5. True
6. False; consolation
7. False; it is a sign that God is preparing us to receive better gifts

8. True
9. False; Acedia
10. False; The Lord's Prayer/The Our Father

Final Exam

Matching

2 points each

1. O
2. V
3. H
4. D
5. B
6. W
7. P
8. F
9. J
10. A
11. M
12. G
13. U
14. R
15. K
16. X
17. I
18. L
19. C
20. N
21. Y
22. Q
23. S
24. T
25. E

Short Answer

5 Points Each

1. What questions does the creation account in Genesis seek to answer? What questions does it not seek to answer?

The creation account in Genesis seeks to answer questions about the religious truth of creation and the religious truth about man. It does not seek to answer questions about science or history.

2. What does it mean for man to be a steward of creation?

Being a steward of creation means exercising dominion over the world, acting as caretakers so that others can enjoy the fruits of creation and so that we can offer all the goods of creation back to God in thanksgiving.

3. Why does the Church call Jesus the "New Adam" and Mary the "New Eve"?

The Church calls Jesus the "New Adam" because, just as sin came into the world through one man, Adam, so salvation comes through the obedience of one man, Jesus.

The Church calls Mary the "New Eve" because, similar to how Adam's sin occurred through the help of Eve, Jesus's work of salvation occurs with the cooperation of Mary.

4. Name two ways Baptism was prefigured in the Old Covenant.

Possible Answers: Baptism was prefigured in the Old Covenant in the Flood, circumcision, and the deliverance of God's people through the parting of the Red Sea.

5. What does the angel Gabriel mean when he calls Mary "full of grace"?

When the angel Gabriel calls Mary "full of grace" he means that she is free from sin so that she could bring Jesus into the world.

6. What is a parable? Give one example of a parable used by Jesus in the Gospels.

A parable is a simple image or comparison, often told through a story, that reveals some aspect of the kingdom. Examples include the parable of the mustard seed, the parable of the leaven, the parable of the weed among the weeds, the parable of the hidden treasure, the parable of the pearl of great price, and the parable of the sower.

7. What are the four last things? Give a short description of each.

Death, judgment, heaven, and hell are the four last things. Death is the separation of the soul from the body. Judgment is how we will give an account to God for how we've responded to his grace. Heaven is a communion of life and love with the Holy Trinity, Mary, and all the saints and angels. Heaven is the fulfillment of all our desires and the state of supreme happiness. Hell is the separation from God caused by our own free choice to reject God's mercy.

8. How do we know, based on Scripture, that Jesus wasn't speaking metaphorically when he said that we must eat his flesh and drink his blood?

We know, based on Scripture, that Jesus wasn't speaking metaphorically when he said that we must eat his flesh and drink his blood because in John 3:3–7 when Nicodemus objected to Jesus saying that one must be "born again," Jesus clarified his symbolic meaning from the literal meaning of his words. He does not do so anywhere in John 6, and in fact, "doubles down" on his words, repeating them more emphatically.

9. What are the three theological virtues? Give a short definition of each.

The three theological virtues are faith, hope, and love (or charity). Faith is the theological virtue by which we believe in God, in all that he has said and revealed to us, and in all that his Church proposes for our belief. Hope is the theological virtue by which we desire the kingdom of heaven and eternal life as our happiness, placing our trust in Christ's promises and relying not on our own strength, but on the help of the grace of the Holy Spirit. Charity is the theological virtue by which we love God above all things for his own sake, and our neighbor as ourselves for the love of God.

10. What does "ongoing conversion" mean?

"Ongoing conversion" means that we don't just choose to follow Christ for once and for all: throughout our lives we must continue to mature and grow in our faith.